The Irish Get Up an

ISBN 978-1-9109

Published in Irel
GET UP AND GO PUB
Cambolíne, Hazelwood, Sligo,
Email: info@getupandgodiary.com
www.getupandgodiary.com

Compiled by Eileen Forrestal
Graphic design by Nuala Redmond
Illustrations: dreamstime.com; shutterstock.com
Printed in Ireland by GPS Colour Graphics.

*Let us go forth, the tellers of tales,
and seize whatever prey the heart longs
for, and have no fear. Everything exists,
everything is true, and the earth is only
a little dust under our feet.*
WB Yeats

Copyright c 2007-2018 Get Up And Go Publications Ltd.

All right reserved. No part of this publication may be reproduced, stored in, or introduced into, a retrieval system, or transmitted in any form, or by any means (electronic, mechanical, scanning, recording or otherwise) without the prior permission of the Publisher. Any person who does any unauthorised act in relation to this publication may be liable to criminal prosecution and civil claim for damages.

2018 BANK AND PUBLIC HOLIDAYS

REPUBLIC OF IRELAND
New Year's Day, 1 January;
St Patrick's Day Bank Holiday, 19 March;
Good Friday, 30 March;
Easter Monday, 2 April;
May Day Bank Holiday, 7 May;
June Bank Holiday, 4 June;
August Bank Holiday, 6 August;
October Bank Holiday, 29 October;
Christmas Day, 25 December;
St Stephen's Day, 26 December.

NORTHERN IRELAND
New Year's Day, 1 January;
Good Friday, 30 March;
May Day Holiday, 7 May;
Orangemen's Holiday, 12 July;
Christmas Day, 25 December;
St Patrick's Day, 19 March;
Easter Monday, 2 April;
Spring Bank Holiday, 28 May;
Summer Bank Holiday, 27 August;
Boxing Day, 26 December.

ENGLAND, SCOTLAND AND WALES
New Year's Day, 1 January;
Easter Monday, 2 April;
Spring Bank Holiday, 28 May;
Christmas Day, 25 December;
Good Friday, 30 March;
May Day Holiday, 7 May;
Summer Bank Holiday, 27 August;
Boxing Day, 26 December.

UNITED STATES OF AMERICA
New Year's Day, 1 January;
Presidents' Day, 19 February;
Independence Day, 4 July;
Columbus Day, 8 October;
Thanksgiving Day, 22 November;
Martin Luther King Day, 15 January;
Memorial Day, 28 May;
Labour Day, 3 September;
Veterans Day, 11 November;
Christmas Day, 25 December.

CANADA
New Year's Day, 1 January;
Heritage Day, 19 February;
St Patrick's Day, 19 March;
Easter Monday, 2 April;
Canada Day, 1 July;
Thanksgiving Day, 8 October;
Christmas Day, 25 December;
Family Day, 19 February;
Commonwealth Day, 12 March;
Good Friday, 30 March;
Victoria Day 21 May;
Labour Day, 3 September;
Remembrance Day, 11 November;
Boxing Day, 26 December.

AUSTRALIA (NATIONAL HOLIDAYS)
New Year's Day, 1 January;
Good Friday, 30 March;
Anzac Day 25 April;
Christmas Day, 25 December;
Australia Day, 26 January;
Easter Monday, 2 April;
Queen's Birthday, 1 October;
Boxing Day, 26 December.

2018 CALENDAR

JANUARY
Mon	Tue	Wed	Thu	Fri	Sat	Sun
1	2	3	4	5	6	7
8	9	10	11	12	13	14
15	16	17	18	19	20	21
22	23	24	25	26	27	28
29	30	31				

FEBRUARY
Mon	Tue	Wed	Thu	Fri	Sat	Sun
			1	2	3	4
5	6	7	8	9	10	11
12	13	14	15	16	17	18
19	20	21	22	23	24	25
26	27	28				

MARCH
Mon	Tue	Wed	Thu	Fri	Sat	Sun
			1	2	3	4
5	6	7	8	9	10	11
12	13	14	15	16	17	18
19	20	21	22	23	24	25
26	27	28	29	30	31	

APRIL
Mon	Tue	Wed	Thu	Fri	Sat	Sun
						1
2	3	4	5	6	7	8
9	10	11	12	13	14	15
16	17	18	19	20	21	22
23	24	25	26	27	28	29
30						

MAY
Mon	Tue	Wed	Thu	Fri	Sat	Sun
	1	2	3	4	5	6
7	8	9	10	11	12	13
14	15	16	17	18	19	20
21	22	23	24	25	26	27
28	29	30	31			

JUNE
Mon	Tue	Wed	Thu	Fri	Sat	Sun
				1	2	3
4	5	6	7	8	9	10
11	12	13	14	15	16	17
18	19	20	21	22	23	24
25	26	27	28	29	30	

JULY
Mon	Tue	Wed	Thu	Fri	Sat	Sun
						1
2	3	4	5	6	7	8
9	10	11	12	13	14	15
16	17	18	19	20	21	22
23	24	25	26	27	28	29
30	31					

AUGUST
Mon	Tue	Wed	Thu	Fri	Sat	Sun
		1	2	3	4	5
6	7	8	9	10	11	12
13	14	15	16	17	18	19
20	21	22	23	24	25	26
27	28	29	30	31		

SEPTEMBER
Mon	Tue	Wed	Thu	Fri	Sat	Sun
					1	2
3	4	5	6	7	8	9
10	11	12	13	14	15	16
17	18	19	20	21	22	23
24	25	26	27	28	29	30

OCTOBER
Mon	Tue	Wed	Thu	Fri	Sat	Sun
1	2	3	4	5	6	7
8	9	10	11	12	13	14
15	16	17	18	19	20	21
22	23	24	25	26	27	28
29	30	31				

NOVEMBER
Mon	Tue	Wed	Thu	Fri	Sat	Sun
			1	2	3	4
5	6	7	8	9	10	11
12	13	14	15	16	17	18
19	20	21	22	23	24	25
26	27	28	29	30		

DECEMBER
Mon	Tue	Wed	Thu	Fri	Sat	Sun
					1	2
3	4	5	6	7	8	9
10	11	12	13	14	15	16
17	18	19	20	21	22	23
24	25	26	27	28	29	30
31						

Forgive the past – let it go
Live the present – the power of now
Create the future – thoughts become things

Dear Reader,

We are delighted that you are holding this Irish Get Up and Go Diary 2018 in your hands today. You are about to embark on a wonderful journey with 'the world's best loved transformational diary'.

Whether you have chosen this diary for yourself or received it as a gift from a friend, we know it will provide the inspiration, encouragement, motivation and empowerment you need as you progress towards fulfilling your goals and dreams in 2018.

If you would like to connect with our growing Get Up and Go community, we invite you to visit our website **www.getupandgodiary.com** where you can follow our blog, find out about our new products, plus details of special offers and upcoming Get Up and Go events.

You may also like to follow us on Facebook, Twitter or Instagram for additional words of inspiration and encouragement.

Whether this is your first Get Up and Go Diary or you are a regular and loyal customer we thank you and trust that you will benefit from the words of wisdom contained therein. We would love you to share the value of the Get Up and Go Diaries with your family and friends.

Best wishes for the year ahead!
Sincerely,
Eileen, Brendan, and the Get Up and Go team

This diary belongs to: _____

Address: _____

Tel: _____ Email: _____

EMERGENCY TELEPHONE NUMBERS

_____

_____

SPRIOCANNA
GOALS

EANÁIR
JANUARY

Is maith an scáthán súil chara.
A friend's eye is a good mirror.

Do not wait to strike till the iron is hot; but make it hot by striking.
WB Yeats

A good retreat is better than a bad stand.
Irish proverb

JANUARY

> You're off to great places!
> Today is your day!
> Your mountain is waiting,
> So – get on your way!
> — Dr Seuss

The most useful piece of learning is to unlearn what is untrue.
— Antisthenes

Always remember to forget
The troubles that passed away.
But never forget to remember
The blessings that come each day.

You can't cross the sea merely by standing and staring at the water.
— Rabindranath Tagore

Happy New Year!

MONDAY 1
HAPPY NEW YEAR!

Wipe the slate clean – erase all your resentments

There is only one time that is important – NOW! It is the most important time because it is the only time that we have any power.
Leo Tolstoy

There are far, far better things ahead than any we leave behind.
CS Lewis

TUESDAY 2

Practice generous listening

WEDNESDAY 3

Be grateful that you are you

THURSDAY 4

Think positive thoughts

FRIDAY 5

However good or bad the situation is, it will change

JANUARY

For the only safe harbour in this life's tossing, troubled sea is to refuse to be bothered about what the future will bring and to stand ready and confident, squaring the breast to take without skulking or flinching whatever fortune hurls at us.

Seneca

When another person makes you suffer, it is because he suffers deeply within himself, and his suffering is spilling over. He does not need punishment; he needs help. That's the message he is sending.

Thích Nhat Hanh

In the realm of ideas, everything depends on enthusiasm. In the real world, all rests on perseverance.

Johann Wolfgang von Goethe

SATURDAY **6**

Passion in life comes from having a purpose

SUNDAY **7**

Don't hurt anyone intentionally, even yourself

THE PARADOX OF OUR AGE

We have bigger houses but smaller families; more conveniences, but less time.

We have more degrees but less sense; more knowledge but less judgment; more experts, but more problems; more medicines but less healthiness.

We've been all the way to the moon and back, but have trouble in crossing the street to meet our new neighbour.

We built more computers to hold more copies than ever, but have less real communication; We have become long on quantity, but short on quality.

These are times of fast foods but slow digestion; Tall men but short characters; Steep profits but shallow relationships.

It's a time when there is much in the window, but nothing in the room.

Dalai Lama

Let us then be what we are, and speak what we think, and in all things keep ourselves loyal to truth.

Henry Wadsworth Longfellow

JANUARY

MONDAY 8

Keep your mind's eye firmly on what you want to achieve

TUESDAY 9

Keep focused on the bigger picture

Consult not your fears, but your hopes and dreams. Think not about your frustrations, but about your unfilled potential. Concern yourself not with what you tried and failed in, but what is still possible for you to do.

Pope John XXIII

The cure for anything is salt water: sweat, tears or the sea.

Isak Dinesen

We tend to forget that happiness doesn't come as a result of getting something we don't have, but rather of recognising and appreciating what we do have.

Frederick Koenig

In a world of grief and pain, flowers bloom, even then.

Kobayashi Issa

WEDNESDAY 10

Be quick to praise and slow to criticise

THURSDAY 11

Accept criticism as simply another view

FRIDAY 12

Thank someone who helped you

SATURDAY 13

It's easier to be kind

SUNDAY 14

Don't indulge in unnecessary drama

JANUARY

MONDAY 15

Miracles come in moments, be ready and willing

TUESDAY 16

A clear conscience makes a comfortable pillow

Once you start to awaken, no one can ever claim you again for the old patterns. Now you realise how precious your time here is. You are no longer willing to squander your essence on undertakings that do not nourish your true self; your patience grows thin with tired talk and dead language.
John O'Donohue

All the world's a stage and most of us are desperately unrehearsed.
Sean O'Casey

WEDNESDAY 17

Work through any fears you may have

What are the proper grounds for joy? Is it circumstance which will determine the stature of my spirit? Ah, no. It is choice. It is always a choice – in the face of any event – for joy.
Mary Anne Radmacher

Your life does not get better by chance, it gets better by change.
Jim Rohn

THURSDAY 18

You are more capable than you know

FRIDAY 19

Do the things you don't like doing first

SATURDAY 20

Share your blessings

SUNDAY 21

Love changes everything

JANUARY

Have patience with everything unresolved in your heart and try to love the questions themselves as if they were locked rooms or books written in a very foreign language. Don't search for the answers, which could not be given to you now, because you would not be able to live them. And the point is to live everything. Live the questions now. Perhaps then, someday far in the future, you will gradually, without even noticing it, live your way into the answer.

Rainer Maria Rilke

The breaking of a wave cannot explain the whole sea.
Vladimir Nabokov

Stop acting as if life is a rehearsal. Live this day as if it were your best. The past is over and gone. The future is not guaranteed.

MONDAY 22

You are doing a great job

TUESDAY 23

Acceptance is the route to happiness

> Judgements prevent us from seeing the good that lies beyond appearances.
> *Wayne Dyer*

WEDNESDAY 24

Never give up on anybody

THURSDAY 25

You cannot live other people's lives for them

FRIDAY 26

Eliminate self-defeating self-talk

SATURDAY 27

Be enthusiastic about your life purpose

SUNDAY 28

Grant yourself permission to be yourself

MONDAY 29

Be willing to make promises

TUESDAY 30

Deal with life from what is possible

WEDNESDAY 31

Be open to miracles

RULES FOR HAPPINESS
Something to do,
Someone to love,
Something to hope for.

Immanuel Kant

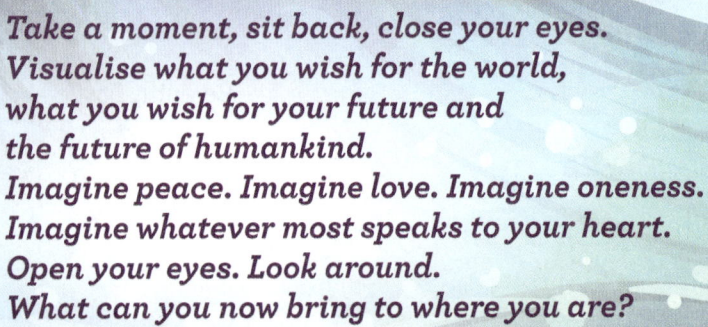

Take a moment, sit back, close your eyes.
Visualise what you wish for the world,
what you wish for your future and
the future of humankind.
Imagine peace. Imagine love. Imagine oneness.
Imagine whatever most speaks to your heart.
Open your eyes. Look around.
What can you now bring to where you are?
Are you willing to be what you can see?

Ar scáth a chéile a mhaireann na daoine.

People live in one another's shadows.

The hallway of every man's life is paced with pictures; pictures gay and pictures gloomy, all useful, for if we be wise, we can learn from them a richer and braver way to live.

Sean O'Casey

A questioning man is halfway to being wise.

Irish proverb

spriocanna

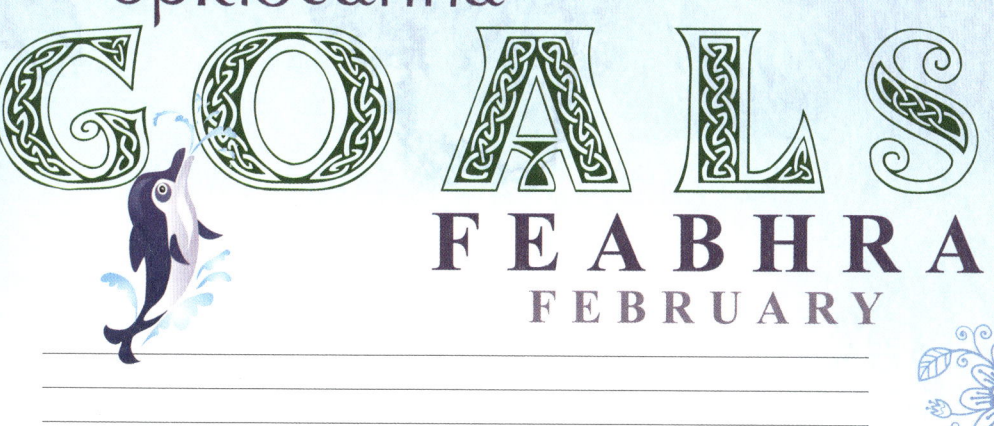

GOALS

FEABHRA
FEBRUARY

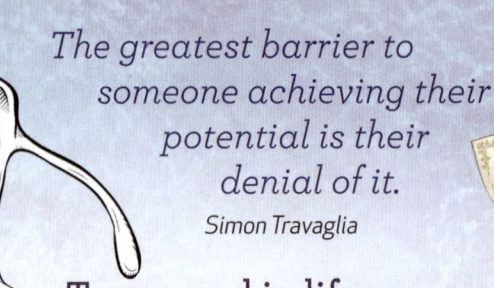

The greatest barrier to someone achieving their potential is their denial of it.
Simon Travaglia

To succeed in life, you need three things: a wishbone, a backbone and a funny bone.
Reba McEntire

THURSDAY **1**

Avoid making judgement

We are all in the gutter, but some of us are looking to the stars.

When a man looks at the stars, he grows calm and forgets small things. They answer his questions and show him that his earth is only one of the million worlds. Hold your soul still and look upward often, and you will understand their speech. Never forget the stars.
Frances Hodgson Burnett

FEBRUARY

Live your dreams.
You are loved.
You are wonderfully made.
You are beautiful.
You have purpose.
You are a masterpiece.
God has a great plan for you.
The tragedy in life doesn't lie in not reaching your goal.
The tragedy lies in having no goal to reach.

Benjamin Mays

Anyone can hold the helm when the sea is calm.

Publilius Syrus

Follow your Dream

FRIDAY 2

It takes courage to speak your truth

SATURDAY 3

It is your thinking that has you think what you think

SUNDAY 4

This day will not come around again

With realisation of one's own potential and self-confidence in one's ability, one can build a better world.
Tenzin Gyatso

Start living now.
Stop saving the good china
for that special occasion.
Stop withholding your love
until that special person materialises.
Every day you are alive is a special occasion.
Every minute, every breath, is a gift from God.
Mary Manin Morrissey

Listen to successful people when they give you advice, and know that nothing can be achieved in the same way twice.

If you are still searching for that one person who will change your life, take a look in the mirror.
Unknown Author

FEBRUARY

> If you run into a wall, don't turn around and give up. Figure out how to climb it, go through it, or work around it.
>
> *Michael Jordan*

MONDAY 5

Keep it simple

TUESDAY 6

Smile before you speak – it has a magical effect on the words you say

WEDNESDAY 7

Take time to consider your options

> *Only by giving are you able to receive more than you already have.*
>
> *Jim Rohn*

FEBRUARY

THURSDAY 8

Notice something today you didn't notice yesterday

FRIDAY 9

If in doubt, honour your word.

SATURDAY 10

There is a wisdom in every moment

> How inappropriate to call this planet Earth, when it is clearly Ocean.
> *Arthur C Clarke*

> *Live out of your imagination, not your history.*
> Stephen Covey

SUNDAY 11

Resist the need to be right

Share your heart as deeply as you can reach.
Mary Anne Radmacher

MONDAY **12**

Be passionately curious about the world

TUESDAY **13**

Use your imagination for good

WEDNESDAY **14**
St Valentine's Day

Worry less and dream more

THURSDAY **15**

Cherish your freedoms

A flower does not think of competing with the flower next to it. It just blooms.
Sensei Ogui

FEBRUARY

When the eyes and the ears are open,
even the leaves on the trees teach like
pages from the scriptures.

Kabir

FRIDAY 16

Choices have consequences

SATURDAY 17

To grow we must change

SUNDAY 18

Trust in the goodness of others

The greatest gift you can give someone is your time. Because when you give your time, you are giving a portion of your life that you will never get back.

When we hit our lowest point, we are open to the greatest change.

Overcome greed with generosity,
Overcome anger with loving kindness,
Overcome ignorance with understanding.
      Heart of Buddha

MONDAY **19**

You are the hero of your own story

TUESDAY **20**

There is something to learn today

WEDNESDAY **21**

Do not rush to judgement

THURSDAY **22**

Life isn't fair, and it's not personal!

A person who lives within their means suffers from a lack of imagination.
      Oscar Wilde

You change the world by being yourself and doing what you do.
Yoko Ono

FRIDAY 23

Don't take yourself so seriously, no one else does

SATURDAY 24

Develop a partnership win-win mindset

SUNDAY 25

When in doubt just take the next small step

When we rip the shackles of 'money' from our wrists, our minds become clear and we see what truly makes us happy. We spend more time with friends and family. We focus on our passions and hobbies. In essence, we get back to the foundation of what it means to be human. After all, none of us will ever arrive upon the mountain of our last moments of existence wishing we spent more time working at the office. We will instead arrive wishing we completed that book, that painting or that experience with those we love most. For those can be purchased not with money, but with time. And there is no more cunning, covert and deceitful thief of time as that villain we call money.

FEBRUARY

> May your dreams be larger than mountains and may you have the courage to scale their summits.
> *Harley King*

> It is better to have a short life that is full of doing what you love, than to have a long life doing something you hate.
> *Alan Watts*

> This world is but a canvas to our imagination.
> *Henry David Thoreau*

MONDAY 26

Everything can change in the blink of an eye

TUESDAY 27

Be grateful for everything

WEDNESDAY 28

Have the courage to admit your mistakes

spriocanna
GOALS
MÁRTA
MARCH

_____
_____
_____
_____
_____
_____
_____
_____

Chíonn beirt rud nach bhfeiceann duine amháin.
Two people see a thing that an individual does not see.

Every eye forms its own fancy.
Irish proverb

Life is a journey that must be travelled no matter how bad the roads and accommodations.
Oliver Goldsmith

DUST IF YOU MUST

Dust if you must, but wouldn't it be better
To paint a picture, or write a letter,
Bake a cake, or plant a seed;
Ponder the difference between want and need?

Dust if you must, but there's not much time,
With rivers to swim, and mountains to climb;
Music to hear, and books to read;
Friends to cherish, and life to lead.

Dust if you must, but the world's out there
With the sun in your eyes, and the wind in your hair;
A flutter of snow, a shower of rain,
This day will not come around again.

Dust if you must, but bear in mind,
Old age will come and it's not kind.
And when you go (and go you must)
You, yourself, will make more dust.

Rose Milligan

Your friend is your needs answered.
He is your field which you sow with love
and reap with thanksgiving.
And he is your board and your fireside.
For you come to him with your hunger,
and you seek him for peace.
Kahlil Gibran

THURSDAY **1**

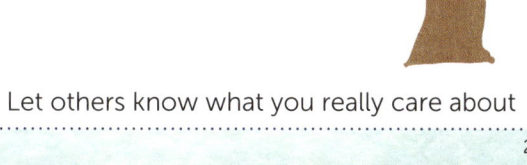

Let others know what you really care about

MARCH

The effect of life in society is to complicate and confuse our existence, making us forget what we really are by causing us to become obsessed with what we are not.
Zhuangzi

My mother-in-law said, 'One day I will dance on your grave.' I said 'I hope you do; I will be buried at sea.'
Les Dawson

So we shall let the reader answer this question for herself: who is the happier, those who have braved the storm of life and lived or those who stay securely on the shore and merely exist?

It had long since come to my attention that people of accomplishment rarely sat back and let things happen to them. They went out and happened to things.
Leonardo da Vinci

FRIDAY 2

Forget blame and fault, look for solutions

SATURDAY 3

Never allow one dispute to injure a friendship

The best people possess a feeling for beauty, the courage to take risks, the discipline to tell the truth, the capacity for sacrifice. Ironically, their virtues make them vulnerable; they are often wounded, sometimes destroyed.
Ernest Hemingway

LOVE LETTERS TO YOURSELF

This is taken from a love letter
(a gentle reminder)
I wrote to myself recently.
Live in your joy today.
Be authentic. Love yourself. First.
Love others from your own abundance.
Life Changes. Circumstances change.
Sometimes you try to fit your old way
of being into new circumstances
rather than becoming new yourself.
Embrace transformation as an opportunity.
And keep on writing love letters to yourself.
Mary Anne Radmacher

As human beings, our greatness lies not so much in being able to remake the world – that is the myth of the atomic age – as in being able to remake ourselves.
Gandhi

SUNDAY **4**

Share the love that lives within you

If you are silent, be silent out of love.
If you speak, speak out of love.
St Augustine

MONDAY 5

Direct your energy towards the things that truly matter

The purpose of life is to live it, to taste experience to the utmost, to reach out eagerly and without fear for newer and richer experience.
Eleanor Roosevelt

TUESDAY 6

Learn from the mistakes of others

WEDNESDAY 7

Right now you have great power to do something wonderful

THURSDAY 8

Don't shoot the messenger

MARCH

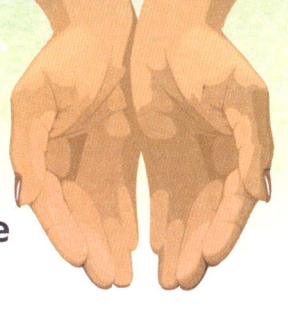

Friends share our pain and touch our wounds with a gentle and tender hand.

Henri Nouwen

Don't be afraid of new beginnings. Don't shy away from new people, new energy, new surroundings. Embrace new chances at happiness.

Billy Chapata

A child has no trouble believing the unbelievable nor does the genius of the madman. It is only you and I with our big brains, and our tiny hearts, who doubt and overthink and hesitate.

FRIDAY 9

Get rid of anything that is not useful, beautiful or joyful

SATURDAY 10

Don't weigh yourself down with judgements

SUNDAY 11
Mother's Day

Be your very best today

MARCH

OPTIMIST: Someone who figures that taking a step backward after taking a step forward is not a disaster, it's more like a cha-cha.

MONDAY 12

Plan for success

> **Keep a green tree in your heart and perhaps a singing bird will come.**
> Chinese Proverb

Strength does not come from winning. Your struggles develop your strengths. When you go through hardships and decide not to surrender, that is strength.
Mahatma Gandhi

Even the upper end of the river believes in the ocean.
William Stafford

TUESDAY 13

Your beliefs shape your thoughts

> If you want to build a ship, don't drum up people together to collect wood and don't assign them tasks and work, but rather teach them to long for the endless immensity of the sea.
>
> *Antoine de Saint-Exupery*

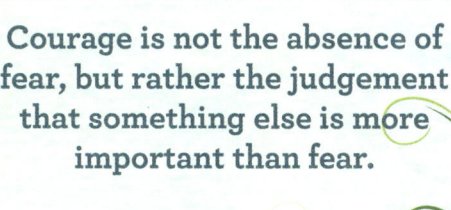

WEDNESDAY 14

Clear out the clutter

THURSDAY 15

Spend time with enthusiastic people

FRIDAY 16

The world is the way it is

> *The man who moves a mountain begins by carrying away small stones.*
>
> Confucius

> Courage is not the absence of fear, but rather the judgement that something else is more important than fear.

MARCH

SATURDAY 17
Happy 🍀 St. Patricks Day

The truth will set you free

Wherever you go and whatever you do, May the luck of the Irish be there with you.

You cannot help the poor by destroying the rich. You cannot strengthen the weak by weakening the strong. You cannot bring about prosperity by discouraging thrift. You cannot lift the wage earner up by pulling the wage payer down. You cannot further the brotherhood of man by inciting class hatred. You cannot build character and courage by taking away people's initiative and independence. You cannot help people permanently by doing for them, what they could and should do for themselves.

Abraham Lincoln

SUNDAY 18

Acknowledge the gifts in your life

The best way to treat obstacles is to use them as stepping-stones. Laugh at them, tread on them, and let them lead you to something better.

Enid Blyton

MONDAY 19

Don't worry too much about what other people think

TUESDAY 20

You can have results or excuses

WEDNESDAY 21

Accepting responsibility for your life is the key to personal freedom

THURSDAY 22

Fear is nothing more than a state of mind

FRIDAY 23

We each have more potential that we could ever dream about

MARCH

When I am gone release me, let me go.
I have so many things to see and do.
You must not tie yourself to me with tears.
Be happy that we had our precious years.
I gave you all my love ... now you can guess
How much you gave to me in happiness.
I thank you for the love that you have shown,
But it is time I travel on alone.
So grieve a while for me if grieve you must,
Then let your grief be comforted by trust.
It's only for a while that we must part,
So bless the memories within your heart.
I won't be far away as life goes on,
So if you need me, call and I will come.
Though you can't see or touch me I'll be near
And if you listen with your heart, you'll hear
All of my love around you soft and clear.
And then when you must come this way alone,
I'll greet you with a smile and take you home.

SATURDAY 24

Life would be dull without human error

SUNDAY 25

Pay attention to what matters

Life is like a game of cards. The hand that is dealt to you represents determinism; the way you play it is free will.
Jawaharlal Nehru

Good decisions are a consequence of experience and experience is a consequence of bad decisions.

Change is always happening for the good of you and for everyone. It is the evolution of life. In matters of style, swim with the current; in matters of principle, stand like a rock.
Thomas Jefferson

Everything passes. Everything changes. Just do what you think you should do.
Bob Dylan

MONDAY 26

Only that which is honestly got, is gain

TUESDAY 27

Your life is a mirror of your consistent thoughts

WEDNESDAY 28

We all have our own standards and ideals

Our days are happier when we give people a bit of our heart rather than a piece of our mind.

Man suffers only because he takes seriously what the Gods made for fun.
Alan Watts

Life is like an ever-shifting kaleidoscope – a slight change, and all patterns alter.
Sharon Salzberg

THURSDAY 29

There is more pleasure in giving than receiving

FRIDAY 30
Good Friday

Play fair – in love and war

SATURDAY 31

Things are not always as they seem

spriocanna
GOALS

AIBREÁN
APRIL

The world is full of magic things, patiently waiting for our senses to grow sharper.
   — Yeats

_____
_____
_____
_____
_____
_____
_____
_____
_____

A good laugh and a long sleep are the best cures in the doctor's book.
   — Irish proverb

Giorraíonn beirt bóthar.
Two people shorten a road.

SUNDAY **1**
Easter Sunday

Collaboration not competition is key

APRIL

MONDAY 2
Bank holiday

Call home

TUESDAY 3

Look for what is hidden in plain sight

WEDNESDAY 4

Stuff happens

THURSDAY 5

Change your thoughts – change your actions – change your life. Simple

FRIDAY 6

Challenge your assumptions

SATURDAY 7

Your intuition is your inner teacher

SUNDAY 8

Believe in happiness

I PROMISE MYSELF

To be so strong that nothing can disturb my peace of mind. **To talk health**, happiness and prosperity to every person I meet. **To make all my friends feel** that there is something worthwhile in them. **To look at the sunny side** of everything and make my optimism come true. **To think only of the best**, to work only for the best and to expect only the best. **To be just as enthusiastic** about the success of others as I am about my own. **To forget the mistakes** of the past and press on to the greater achievements of the future. **To wear a cheerful expression** at all times and give a smile to every living creature I meet. **To give so much time** to improving myself that I have no time to criticise others. **To be too large for worry**, too noble for anger, too strong for fear and too happy to permit the presence of trouble. **To think well of myself** and to proclaim this fact to the world, not in loud words, but in great deeds. **To live in faith** that the whole world is on my side, so long as I am true to the best that there is in me.

Christian D Larson

Water is the driver of nature.
Leonardo da Vinci

APRIL

Truth exists for the wise, beauty for the feeling heart.

Fredrich Von Schiller

Far and away the best prize that life has to offer is the chance to work hard at work worth doing.

Theodore Roosevelt

MONDAY 9

Spend time alone and get to know yourself

TUESDAY 10

Everyone's opinion is valid – and it's just an opinion

WEDNESDAY 11

Don't worry about what other people think

THURSDAY 12

You are the only adult you are responsible for

> People are capable, at any time in their lives, of doing what they dream of.
> *Paulo Coelho*

FRIDAY 13

Do more of what makes you happy

SATURDAY 14

The universe is an intention fulfilment machine

SUNDAY 15

Dream big

> 'Tis the business of little minds to shrink, but they whose heart is firm, and whose conscience approves their conduct, will pursue their principles unto death.
> *Leonardo da Vinci*

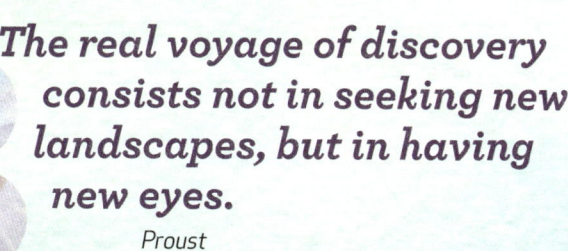

> The real voyage of discovery consists not in seeking new landscapes, but in having new eyes.
> *Proust*

APRIL

Do not take life too seriously.
You will never get out of it alive.
Elbert Hubbard

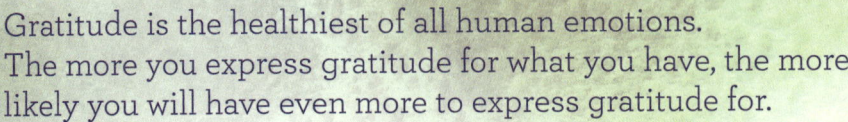

Gratitude is the healthiest of all human emotions. The more you express gratitude for what you have, the more likely you will have even more to express gratitude for.
Zig Ziglar

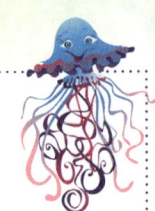

MONDAY 16

Don't put your life on hold – there is no better time than now

TUESDAY 17

It is never too late to change direction

WEDNESDAY 18

Write down what is troubling you then share it to halve it

THURSDAY 19

Review your destination regularly to ensure you are on track

> *'Thank you' is the best prayer that anyone could say. I say that one a lot. Thank you expresses extreme gratitude, humility, understanding.*
>
> Alice Walker

I don't believe in 'thinking' old. Although I've transitioned through many bodies – a baby, toddler, child, teen, young adult, mid-life and older adult – my spirit is unchanged. I support my body with exercise, my mind with reading and writing, and my spirit with the knowing that I am part of the Divine source of all life.

FRIDAY 20

Sing out loud

SATURDAY 21

Be respectful of differences

SUNDAY 22

For good health make enjoyment your wealth

KINDNESS DURING LIFE

I would rather have one little rose
From the garden of a friend,
Than to have the choicest flowers
When my stay on earth must end.
I would rather hear the kindest words
That can now be said to me,
Than flattered when my heart is still
And this life ceased to be.
I would rather have a loving smile
From friends I know are true,
Than tears shed round my casket
When I bid this world adieu.
Bring me any flower today
Be it pink or white or red.
I'd rather have one blossom now
Than a bouquet when I'm dead.

Anon

MONDAY 23

Be a yes to life

TUESDAY 24

Actions speak louder than words

WEDNESDAY 25

Ensure your loved ones feel good about themselves

APRIL

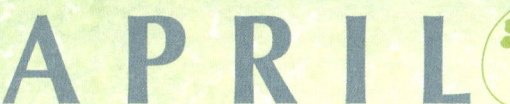

It is a kind of theological folly to suppose that God has made the entire world just for human beings, or to suppose that God is interested in only one of the millions of species that inhabit God's good earth.

Archbishop Desmond Tutu

THURSDAY 26

Thinking is over rated; take an action

FRIDAY 27

No one can keep you down but yourself

SATURDAY 28

Keep your promises

SUNDAY 29

Self acceptance is the beginning of peace

APRIL

Feeling gratitude and not expressing it is like wrapping a present and not giving it.
William Arthur Ward

MONDAY 30

Self expression is essential to life

POSITIVE HABITS OF MINDFUL PEOPLE

- **CURIOUSITY HABIT:** Approach everyday things with curiosity – and savour them.
- **FORGIVENESS HABIT:** Forgive their mistakes – big or small. We have all made mistakes for which we want to be forgiven.
- **GRATITUDE HABIT:** Show gratitude for good moments – and grace for bad ones – and gratitude that we are alive for both.
- **COMPASSION HABIT:** Practice compassion and nurture connections and relatedness with all living creatures.
- **PEACE HABIT:** Make peace with imperfection – inside and out.
- **VULNERABILITY HABIT:** Embrace vulnerability by trusting others – and ourselves.
- **ACCEPTANCE HABIT:** Accept – and appreciate – that things come and go – like the breath.

All the waters run to the sea and yet the sea is not full, and from the place where they began, thither they return again.
Ecclesiastes

spriocanna
GOALS
BEALTAINE
MAY

Ní neart go cur le chéile.
There is no strength without unity.

The work praises the man.
Irish proverb

TUESDAY 1

Expectation can lead to heartache

WEDNESDAY 2

Love as much as you possibly can

MAY

Life does not consist mainly, or even largely, of facts or happenings. It consist mainly of the storm of thoughts that is forever flowing through one's head.
Mark Twain

Every mountain top is within reach if you just keep climbing.

THURSDAY **3**

Grace others with your cheerfulness

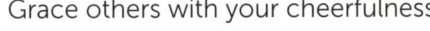

You have to accept whatever comes and the only important thing is that you meet it with courage and with the best that you have to give.
Eleanor Roosevelt

If you aren't in the moment, you are either looking forward to uncertainty, or back to pain and regret.
Jim Carrey

> About morals: I know only that
> what is moral is what you feel good after
> and what is immoral is what you feel bad after.
> *Ernest Hemingway*

FRIDAY 4

Do not worry about that which you cannot control

SATURDAY 5

Notice the beauty in small moments

SUNDAY 6

Spend time with your family

> We live in a wonderful world that is full of beauty, charm and adventure. There is no end to the adventures that we can have if only we seek them with our eyes open.
> Jawaharlal Nehru

> The truth hurts like a thorn at first, but in the end it blossoms like a rose.
> *Samuel Ha-Nagid*

We look and look and look for what we are supposed to learn out of the pain because knowledge is what we're told to find. We are told that pain and suffering has some kind of lesson for us in the trial. But sometimes the lesson isn't the lesson that changes how you function. Sometimes the lesson is this: that even in your torn up, bruised and bloodied self you were strong enough to survive when you didn't think you could.
And that knowledge is a blessing in itself.
Mae-Lex

You can't stop the waves, but you can learn to surf.
Jon Kabat-Zinn

The greater the obstacle, the more glory in overcoming it.
Moliere

We can only be said to be truly alive in those moments when our hearts are conscious of our treasures.
Thornton Wilder

I have accepted fear as a part of life – specifically the fear of change.
I have gone ahead despite the pounding in the heart that says: turn back.
The trouble is, if you don't risk anything, you risk even more.
Erica Jong

MONDAY 7
Bank holiday

You can have the life you want

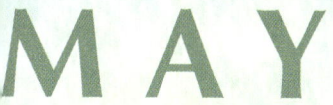

As long as a man stands in his own way, everything seems to be in his way.
Ralph Waldo Emerson

Never give up, for that is just the place and time that the tide will turn.
Harriet Beecher Stowe

TUESDAY 8

Conscious breathing calms the mind

WEDNESDAY 9

In a grown up world, adults need to behave like adults

THURSDAY 10

Don't compare yourself to others

FRIDAY 11

Always focus on the desired outcome

MAY

Wherever there is a human being, there is an opportunity for a kindness.
Seneca

Opportunity dances with those already on the dance floor.
H Jackson Brown Jr

SATURDAY 12

Make peace with your past – it got you here

SUNDAY 13

Choose to be happy

Carpe diem!
Rejoice while you are alive;
enjoy the day; live life to the fullest;
make the most of what you have.
It is later than you think.
Horace

The pursuit of truth and beauty is a sphere of activity in which we are permitted to remain children all our lives.
Albert Einstein

Act as if what you do makes a difference. It does.
William James

If your actions inspire others to dream more, learn more, do more and become more, you are a leader.
John Quincy Adams

Our deepest fear is not that we are inadequate. Our deepest fear is that we are powerful beyond measure. It is our light, not our darkness that most frightens us. We ask ourselves, 'Who am I to be brilliant, gorgeous, talented, fabulous?' Actually, who are you not to be? You are a child of God. Your playing small does not serve the world. There is nothing enlightened about shrinking so that other people won't feel insecure around you. We are all meant to shine, as children do. We were born to make manifest the glory of God that is within us. It's not just in some of us; it's in everyone. And as we let our own light shine, we unconsciously give other people permission to do the same. As we are liberated from our own fear, our presence automatically liberates others.
Marianne Williamson

Where there is great love, there are always miracles. Miracles rest not so much upon faces or voices or healing power from far off, but upon our perceptions being made finer, so that for a moment, our eyes can see and our ears can hear what there is about us always.
Willa Cather

MAY

The study of philosophy is not that we may know what men have thought, but what the truth of things is.
St Thomas Aquinas

Take your shoes off, purred the ocean waves.
Dr SunWolf

MONDAY 14

Live a life of gratitude

TUESDAY 15

Don't impose your values on others

WEDNESDAY 16

Forgive everyone everything

THURSDAY 17

Embrace change, it's already here

> Worry often gives a small thing a big shadow.
> *Swedish Proverb*

> Your inner knowing is your only true compass.
> *Joy Page*

FRIDAY 18

Nurture your self-confidence with every new action

SATURDAY 19

Forgive yourself for past mistakes

SUNDAY 20

Being true to yourself is always the best option

> Happiness is a choice. You grieve, you stomp your feet, you pick yourself up and choose to be happy.
> *Lucy Lawless*

MAY

*Success is a state of mind.
If you want success, start thinking
of yourself as a success.*
Joyce Brothers

*Discipline is the foundation upon
which all success is built. Lack of
discipline inevitably leads to failure.*
Jim Rohn

*It isn't what you have, or who you are,
or where you are, or what you are doing
that makes you happy or unhappy.
It is what you think about.*
Dale Carnegie

MONDAY 21

People just do what they do

TUESDAY 22

Right now is a good time to make a fresh start

WEDNESDAY 23

Honour and appreciate the abundance in your life

> **One must know not just how to accept a gift, but with what grace to share it.**
> *Maya Angelou*

THURSDAY 24

Nobility exists in the soul

FRIDAY 25

We are empowered by empowering others

SATURDAY 26

Only complain to someone who can do something about it

SUNDAY 27

More and bigger is not always better

> **Every art and every enquiry, and similarly every action and choice, is though to aim at some good; and for this reason the good has rightly been declared that at which all things aim.**
> *Aristotle*

MONDAY 28

Believe in yourself and all that you are

TUESDAY 29

Pay who you owe, what you owe, when you owe it

WEDNESDAY 30

Face the future with confidence

THURSDAY 31

Focus on your haves and not on your have nots

Surround yourself with people who take their work seriously, but not themselves, those who work hard and play hard.
Colin Powell

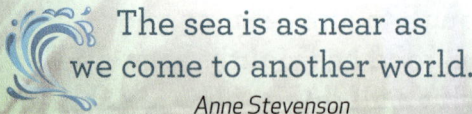

The sea is as near as we come to another world.
Anne Stevenson

spriocanna
GOALS
MEITHEAMH
JUNE

*God made time,
but man made haste.*

Irish proverb

_____
_____
_____
_____
_____
_____
_____
_____

Out of the quarrel with others we make rhetoric;
out of the quarrel with ourselves we make poetry.

WB Yeats

Ná bris do loirgín ar stól
nach bhfuil i do shlí.

*Do not break your shin on a stool
that is not in your way.*

JUNE

> Go confidently in the direction of your dreams. Live the life you have imagined.
> *Henry David Thoreau*

FRIDAY 1

Accept compliments graciously and gracefully

SATURDAY 2

Make amends actively

SUNDAY 3

Your life is your canvas – make it your masterpiece

> **We come this way but once. We can either tiptoe through life and hope we get to death without being badly bruised or we can live a full, complete life achieving our goals and realising our wildest dreams.**
> *Bob Proctor*

Some people come into our lives and quickly go.
Some people stay for awhile,
and move our souls to dance.
They awaken us to a new understanding,
leave footprints on our hearts,
and we are never, ever the same.
Flavia Weedn

Success is not the key to happiness.
Happiness is the key to success.
If you love what you are doing,
you will be successful.
Albert Schweitzer

You will never change your life until
you change something you do daily.
Mike Murdock

We are living in a world of great change and great uncertainty – but also a world of great opportunity.

It was the best of times,
it was the worst of times,
it was the age of wisdom,
it was the age of foolishness,
it was the epoch of belief,
it was the epoch of incredulity,
it was the season of light,
it was the season of darkness,
it was the spring of hope,
it was the winter of despair.
Charles Dickens

JUNE

Your whole past was but a birth and a becoming.
Antoine de Saint-Exupery

Can miles truly separate you from friends? If you want to be with someone you love, aren't you already there!
Richard Bach

MONDAY 4
Bank holiday

Be a good neighbour

TUESDAY 5

Practice visualising what you want – it is very powerful

WEDNESDAY 6

There is no 'no' in life

THURSDAY 7

Respond promptly to your calls and emails

> *Those who flow as life flows
> know they need no other force.*
> Lao Tzu

FRIDAY **8**

End the struggle and dance with life

SATURDAY **9**

A helping hand is better than good advice

SUNDAY **10**

The joker will be the winner in the end

> **Like failure, chaos contains information that can lead to knowledge – even wisdom.**
> Toni Morrison

We are mosaics. Pieces of light, love, history, stars, glued together with magic and music and words.
Anita Krizzan

Fair weather never made a good sailor.
Unknown

JUNE

MONDAY 11

Keep a sense of perspective – and a sense of humour

TUESDAY 12

Create an inspiration board and allow yourself to be inspired

WEDNESDAY 13

Ask for support when you need it

THURSDAY 14

It is not always about you

FRIDAY 15

Acknowledge yourself for all you have accomplished

> *Positive thinking will let you do everything better than negative thinking will.*
> Zig Ziglar

I'm 36 and I have so many unanswered questions.
I still haven't found out who let the dogs out...
How to get to Sesame Street...
Why Dora doesn't just use Google Maps...
Why do all flavours of fruit loops taste exactly the same...
How do they get the figs into the fig rolls...
Why does Donald Duck wear a towel after a shower,
    yet never wears pants...
Why eggs are packaged in a flimsy paper carton,
    but batteries are secured in plastic that's tough as nails,
    and light bulbs are also in a flimsy carton...
Ever buy scissors? You need scissors to cut
    into the packaging of scissors!
I still don't understand why there is braille on drive up ATMs
    or why "abbreviated" is such a long word,
    or why is there a D in 'fridge' but not in refrigerator...
Why lemon juice is made with artificial flavour,
    yet dish-washing liquid is made with real lemons...
Why they sterilise the needle for lethal injections...
And, why do you have to 'put your two cents in',
    but it's only a 'penny for your thoughts'?
    Where's that extra penny going to?
Why do 'The Alphabet Song' and
    'Twinkle Twinkle Little Star'
    have the same tune?
And why did you just try to sing those two previous songs?
There are so many unanswered questions in life.

> I remind myself every morning:
> Nothing I say this day will teach me anything.
> So if I'm going to learn, I must do it by listening.
> *Larry King*

JUNE

Let the beauty of what you love be what you do.
Rumi

SATURDAY 16

Have a bath by candlelight

SUNDAY 17
Father's Day

Never say never

You can't keep the birds of sadness from flying over your head, but you can keep them from nesting in your hair.
Sharon Creech

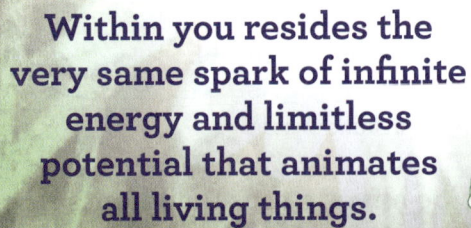

Within you resides the very same spark of infinite energy and limitless potential that animates all living things.
Panache Desai

Reflect upon your present blessings, of which every man has plenty; not on your past misfortunes, of which all men have some.
Charles Dickens

MONDAY **18**

Do what you can to make your world a better place

TUESDAY **19**

No one can be grateful and unhappy at the same time

WEDNESDAY **20**

Get rid of stuff you don't need

THURSDAY **21**

Enjoy healthy food

We must free ourselves of the hope that the sea will ever rest. We must learn to sail in high winds.
Aristotle Onassis

We can only be said to be alive in those moments when our hearts are conscious of our treasures.
Thornton Wilder

> Our goals can only be reached through a vehicle of a plan, in which we must fervently believe, and upon which we must vigorously act. There is no other route to success.
>
> *Pablo Picasso*

FRIDAY 22

Go outdoors into nature and observe the peace and pace of life unfolding

SATURDAY 23

Fix the problem not the blame

SUNDAY 24

If you speak kind words, you will hear kind echoes

Deep peace of the quiet earth to you, who, herself unmoving, harbours the movements, and facilitates the life of the ten thousand creatures, while resting contented, stable, tranquil. Deep peace of the quiet earth to you!

JUNE

To see a world in a grain of sand
And a heaven in a wild flower,
Hold infinity in the palm of your hand
And eternity in an hour.
William Blake

MONDAY 25

Your home is your sanctuary

TUESDAY 26

Your true beauty lies in the uniqueness of you

WEDNESDAY 27

Gather strength from life's storms

THURSDAY 28

Put your best foot forward

Is it so bad, then, to be misunderstood?

Pythagoras was misunderstood, and Socrates, and Jesus, and Luther, and Copernicus, and Galileo, and Newton, and every pure and wise spirit that ever took flesh. To be great is to be misunderstood.

Ralph Waldo Emerson

No amount of self-improvement can make up for a lack of self-acceptance.

Anonymous

All children are artists. The problem is how to remain an artist once he grows up.

Pablo Picasso

The fishermen know that the sea is dangerous and the storm terrible, but they have never found these dangers sufficient reason for remaining ashore.

Vincent Van Gogh

FRIDAY 29

Explore the limits of your comfort zone

SATURDAY 30

Feel the fear and do it anyway

spriocanna
GOALS

IÚIL
JULY

Ní dhéanfaidh smaoineamh an treabhadh duit.

You'll never plough a field turning it over in your mind.

People seldom improve when they have no model but themselves to copy after.
Oliver Goldsmith

Continual cheerfulness is a sign of wisdom.
Irish proverb

SUNDAY **1**

Choose your friends carefully

JULY

*Do not regret growing older;
it is a privilege denied to many.*

MONDAY 2

It pays to listen

TUESDAY 3

Plan your next adventure

WEDNESDAY 4

Encourage others

THURSDAY 5

What would someone you admire do in this situation?

FRIDAY 6

You empower your dreams in the pursuit of them

To the people who love you, you are beautiful already. This is not because they're blind to your shortcomings but because they see your soul. Your shortcomings then dim by comparison. The people who care about you are willing to let you be imperfect and beautiful, too.
— Victoria Moran

The trees that are slow to grow bear the best fruit.
— Moliere

It is not in the stars to hold our destiny but in ourselves.

When you have shut your doors, and darkened your room, remember, never to say that you are alone, for you are not alone, but God is within, and your genius is within.
— Epictetus

SATURDAY 7

Develop the talents you have

SUNDAY 8

Bring more fun to your workplace

JULY

If you go looking for a friend, you're going to find they're very scarce. If you go out to be a friend, you'll find them everywhere.
Zig Ziglar

Develop an interest in life as you see it; the people, things, literature, music – the world is so rich, simply throbbing with rich treasures, beautiful souls and interesting people. Forget yourself.
Arthur Miller

Man cannot discover new oceans unless he has the courage to lose sight of the shore.
Andre Gide

The way to develop the best that is in a person is by appreciation and encouragement.
Charles Schwab

MONDAY 9

Master your emotions or they will master you

TUESDAY 10

Accept what you have not yet accepted

WEDNESDAY 11

Beautify your surroundings

> It's easy to judge. It's more difficult to understand. Understanding requires compassion, patience, and a willingness to believe that good hearts sometimes choose poor methods. Through judging, we separate. Through understanding, we grow.
>
> *Doe Zantamata*

THURSDAY 12

Say yes to opportunity

FRIDAY 13

Do what you know to do

SATURDAY 14

Always look for the diamond in the charcoal

SUNDAY 15

Don't look back, you're not going that way

JULY

Sometimes even to live is an act of courage.

Lucius Annaeus Seneca

MONDAY 16

Be prepared for surprises

TUESDAY 17

Listen to the music in your heart

WEDNESDAY 18

Measure your success by your level of happiness

THURSDAY 19

Notice the beauty that surrounds you

Human beings can alter their lives by altering their attitudes of mind.

William James

Whatever you do, you need courage. Whatever course you decide upon, there is always someone to tell you that you are wrong. There are always difficulties arising that tempt you to believe your critics are right.

Ralph Waldo Emerson

FRIDAY 20

What did you want to be when you grew up?

SATURDAY 21

You are the master of your fate

SUNDAY 22

Stay open and curious

Truth is beautiful without doubt, but so are lies.

Ralph Waldo Emerson

JULY

But I, being poor, have only my dreams;
I have spread my dreams under your feet;
Tread softly because you tread on my dreams.
WB Yeats

MONDAY 23

Create a life worth loving

For age is opportunity no less
Than youth itself, though in another dress,
And as the evening twilight fades away
The sky is filled with stars, invisible by day.
Henry Wadsworth Longfellow

Accept what is, let go of what was, and have faith in what will be.

To me the sea is a continual miracle;
The fishes that swim – the rocks – the motion
of the waves – the ships, with men in them.
What stranger miracles are there?
Walt Whitman

TUESDAY 24

Happiness is not on the other side of suffering

WEDNESDAY 25

Put your dreams to work for you

THURSDAY 26

What you discover for yourself is yours forever

FRIDAY 27

Take what you do seriously and yourself lightly

SATURDAY 28

Ask the universe for advice

SUNDAY 29

Don't say "I don't care" when it's not true

When 'progress based' thinking dominates a society, who gets left behind?

When the innate wisdom and compassion of artists, poets, teachers, musicians, women, children, elders and animals is treated as inferior and unimportant, who loses out?

Jesus spoke of this, as did the Buddha, Lao Tsu, Gandhi, Helen Keller, Albert Einstein, Mother Theresa, the Dalai Lama, John Lennon, Martin Luther King Jr and countless others down through the ages.

Millions honour and treasure their words, but are we ready yet to become "warriors" of compassion, to put wisdom into action, to open our hearts and question the aggressive thinking that our "great progressive civilisations" continue to perpetuate?

As Einstein said, in order for our species to survive, we may have to.

WHY COMPLICATE LIFE?
Missing somebody? **Call.**
Want to meet up? **Invite.**
Want to be understood? **Explain.**
Have questions? **Ask.**
Don't like something? **Say it.**
Like something? **State it.**
Want or need something? **Ask for it.**
Love someone? **Tell them.**

That is the problem of life.
If we are not fully ourselves,
truly in the present moment,
we miss everything.

Thich Nhat Hanh

JULY

*I find, when you're an optimist,
life has a funny way of looking after you.*
Simon Sinek

MONDAY 30

Every problem has a solution

TUESDAY 31

Browse in a good bookshop

*The true meaning of life is to plant trees,
under whose shade you do not expect to sit.*
Nelson Henderson

Pull out your inner GPS –
It is guided by your intuition.
Set your compass to the four corners.
Going one way is incredibly boring.

Carolyn Riker

Intelligence
without ambition
is a bird
without
wings.

spriocanna
GOALS

LÚNASA
AUGUST

Had I the heavens' embroidered cloths,
Enwrought with golden and silver light,
The blue and the dim and the dark cloths
Of night and light and the half light,
I would spread the cloths under your feet:
But I, being poor, have only my dreams;
I have spread my dreams under your feet;
Tread softly because you tread on my dreams.
WB Yeats

*Always remember to forget
The things that made you sad.
But never forget to remember
The things that made you glad.*
Irish proverb

Cleachtadh a dhéanann maistreacht.

Practice makes mastery.

Above all, watch with glittering eyes the whole world around you, because the greatest secrets are always hidden in the most unlikely places. Those who don't believe in magic will never find it.
Roald Dahl

Don't be too timid and squeamish about your actions. All life is an experiment.
Ralph Waldo Emerson

To love a person is to see all of their magic, and to remind them of it when they have forgotten.

The pessimist complains about the wind; the optimist expects it to change; the realist adjusts the sails.
William Arthur Ward

You are
inspiring
beautiful
courageous
amazing

Knowledge comes from books. Wisdom comes from life.

WEDNESDAY **1**

Reconnect with old friends

AUGUST

There are only two
ways to live your life.
One is as though nothing
is a miracle. The other is
as though everything
is a miracle.

Albert Einstein

So don't be frightened, dear friend,
if a sadness confronts you larger than any
you have ever known, casting its shadow
over all you do. You must think that
something is happening within you, and
remember that life has not forgotten you;
it holds you in its hand and will not let you
fall. Why would you want to exclude from
your life any uneasiness, any pain, any
depression, since you don't know what
work they are accomplishing within you?

Rainer Maria Rilke

**True friends
are never
apart maybe
in distance
but never
in heart.**

Helen Keller

Of life's two chief prizes,
beauty and truth, I found
the first in a loving
heart and the second
in a labourer's hand.

Kahlil Gibran

Try to find someone with a sense of humor. That's an important thing to have because when you get into an argument, one of the best ways to diffuse it is to be funny. You don't want to hide away from a point, because some points are serious, but you'd rather have a discussion that was a discussion, rather than an argument.

Ed Sheeran

Be as simple as you can be. You'll be astonished to see how uncomplicated and happy your life will be.

Paramahansa Yogananda

THURSDAY 2

Listen to those who love you

FRIDAY 3

You are worthy of your love

SATURDAY 4

Build on what you know and be willing to discover something new

SUNDAY 5

You are not what you think you are, but what you think... you are

AUGUST

Instead of comparing our lot with that of those who are more fortunate than we are, we should compare it with the lot of the great majority of our fellow men. It then appears that we are among the privileged.

Helen Keller

MONDAY 6
Bank holiday

Your attitude determines your altitude

TUESDAY 7

Don't be the one holding you back

WEDNESDAY 8

Develop a can-do, will-do mindset

THURSDAY 9

Successful people have successful habits

> The sea! The sea! The open sea!
> The blue, the fresh, the ever free!
>
> *Bryan W Procter*

Hurt people hurt people.
That's how pain gets passed on,
generation after generation.
Break the chain today.
Let the past rest in peace.
Meet anger with understanding.
Fear with compassion.
Judgement with humility.
Criticism with acceptance.
Cruelty with kindness
Greet grimaces with smiles.
Forgive and forget about blame and fault.
Love is the best weapon to shape the future.

Laughter is wine for the soul – laughter soft, or loud and deep, tinged through with seriousness – the hilarious declaration made by man that life is worth living.

We grossly underestimate our capacity for change.

Do you want to meet the love of your life? Look in the mirror.

Byron Katie

AUGUST

RELATIONSHIPS

Accept others the way they are;
   you expect them to accept you as you are.

Don't take other people for granted,
   you don't like to be taken for granted.

Speak the truth from the start –
   you expect others to be truthful with you.

Respect others opinions,
   you want others to respect yours.

Be reliable for doing what you say.

You are responsible for your own happiness;
   don't make others responsible.

Take time to listen to them –
   if you want them to listen to you.

Don't bring up the past –
   you hate it when others do that.

When things get heated, allow things to cool down.

Don't assign blame – we all hate to be blamed.

Look for solutions not evidence.

Act your age at all times;
   adult relationships work better with grown ups.

Let go of comparisons – we hate to be compared.

Give 'the relationship' a vote.

Respect boundaries.

Relationships are a two-way street.

> **There's only one true superpower amongst human beings, and that is being funny. People treat you differently if you can make them laugh.**
> *Jeff Garlin*

FRIDAY 10

Short cuts can often make for long delays

SATURDAY 11

We are attached to our personal view of the world

I have found life an enjoyable, enchanting, active, and sometime terrifying experience, and I've enjoyed it completely. A lament in one ear, maybe, but always a song in the other.
Sean O'C

Life is either a daring adventure or nothing. Security does not exist in nature, nor do the children of men as a whole experience it. Avoiding danger is no safer in the long run than exposure.
Helen Keller

SUNDAY 12

Play more, think less

AUGUST

> The purpose of art is washing the dust of daily life off our souls.
> *Pablo Picasso*

MONDAY 13

You have everything you need

TUESDAY 14

The world is a big place — explore it while you can

WEDNESDAY 15

Give up making the world wrong

THURSDAY 16

If the going gets tough, keep going

> Forgiveness is a funny thing.
> It warms the heart and
> cools the sting.
>
> *William Arthur Ward*

FRIDAY **17**

Go where you are valued

SATURDAY **18**

Maturity is accepting imperfection

> Dwell on the beauty of life. Watch the stars,
> and see yourself running with them.
>
> *Marcus Aurelius*

Every time we walk along a beach, some ancient urge disturbs us so that we find ourselves shedding shoes and garments or scavenging among seaweed and whitened timbers like the homesick refugees of a long war.
Loren Eiseley

SUNDAY **19**

Be your own best friend

> Learn to be thankful for what you already have, while you pursue all that you want.
> *Jim Rohn*

MONDAY **20**

Plan a picnic

TUESDAY **21**

The voice in your head is not always right

WEDNESDAY **22**

In your heart you know

THURSDAY **23**

How you view the world is your choice

AUGUST

I will walk by myself and cure myself in the sunshine and the wind.

Charles Reznikoff

Climb if you will, but remember that courage and strength are nought without prudence, and that a momentary negligence may destroy the happiness of a lifetime. Do nothing in haste; look well to each step; and from the beginning think what may be the end.

Edward Whymper

FRIDAY 24

Don't just go through life, grow and flow through life

SATURDAY 25

Create peace in your mind and your body will reflect it

SUNDAY 26

Deal with unfinished business

MONDAY 27

Don't put limits on your vision

TUESDAY 28

We each dance to the beat of our own drum

WEDNESDAY 29

Life created you to be fulfilled, go to work on that

THURSDAY 30

In the end all that matters is that you loved

> From there to here, and here to there, funny things are everywhere.
> *Dr Seuss*

FRIDAY 31

Don't worry; be happy

Is minic a bhris beál duine a shrón.

It is often that a person's mouth broke his nose.

Spriocanna
GOALS
MEÁN FOMHAIR
SEPTEMBER

As you slide down the banister of life, may the splinters never point the wrong way.

Irish proverb

_____
_____
_____
_____
_____
_____
_____
_____
_____

Write how you want, the critic shall show the world you could have written better.

Oliver Goldsmith

There is a brokenness out of which comes
the unbroken, a shatteredness out of
which blooms the unshatterable.
There is a sorrow beyond all grief
which leads to joy and a fragility out
of whose depths emerges strength.
There is a hollow space too vast for words
through which we pass with each loss, out of
whose darkness we are sanctioned into being.
There is a cry deeper than all sound whose serrated edges
cut the heart as we break open to the place inside which
is unbreakable and whole, while learning to sing.
Rashani

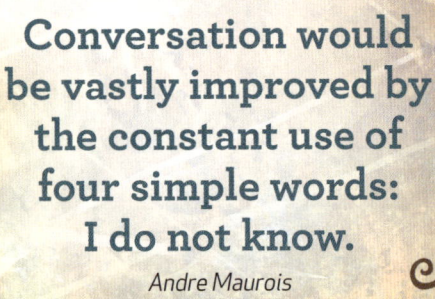

**Conversation would
be vastly improved by
the constant use of
four simple words:
I do not know.**
Andre Maurois

*Two wrongs
don't make a
right, but they
make a good
excuse.*
Thomas Szasz

Comedy is simply a funny way of being serious.
Peter Ustinov

SEPTEMBER

None is more impoverished than the one who has no gratitude. Gratitude is a currency that we can mint for ourselves, and spend without fear of bankruptcy.

Fred De Witt Van Amburgh

SATURDAY 1

Get into the driving seat of your life

SUNDAY 2

A stitch in time saves nine

If you despise the mountains you have climbed, you are not welcomed by the mountains you have not yet climbed!

Mehmet Murat Ildan

Climb the mountains and get their good tidings. Nature's peace will flow into you as sunshine flows into trees. The winds will blow their own freshness into you, and the storms their energy, while cares will drop away from you like the leaves of Autumn.

John Muir

SEPTEMBER

MONDAY 3

Desire is the starting point of all achievement

TUESDAY 4

Give more than is expected of you

WEDNESDAY 5

Be generous with your time and attention

THURSDAY 6

Find something to celebrate today

You cannot escape the responsibility of tomorrow by evading it today.

Abraham Lincoln

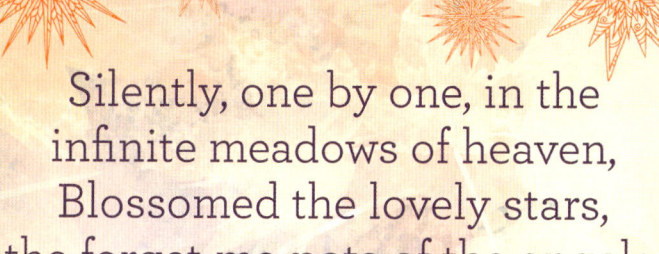

> Silently, one by one, in the
> infinite meadows of heaven,
> Blossomed the lovely stars,
> the forget-me-nots of the angels.
>
> *Henry Wadsworth Longfellow*

Forgiveness is not always easy. At times,
it feels more painful than the wound we suffered,
to forgive the one that inflicted it. And yet,
there is no peace without forgiveness.
Marianne Williamson

FRIDAY 7

Choose to be happy

SATURDAY 8

Courage and confidence grow from within

SUNDAY 9

Most of what you worry about never happens

SEPTEMBER

MONDAY 10

Add value wherever you are

TUESDAY 11

To be heard, speak

WEDNESDAY 12

Life is to be enjoyed, not endured

THURSDAY 13

Meet a friend for lunch

FRIDAY 14

This moment is your greatest point of power

The man who speaks the truth is always at ease.
— Persian Proverb

Be the one who nurtures and builds. Be the one who has an understanding and forgiving heart. Be the one who looks for the best in people. Leave people better than you found them.
— Marvin J Ashton

They deem him their worst enemy who tells them the truth.
— Plato

SATURDAY 15

Value your own wellbeing above all else

SUNDAY 16

Perhaps what you are looking for is right in front of you

*We are all here on earth to help others;
what on earth the others are here for I don't know.*

WH Auden

MONDAY 17

Tomorrow is another day

TUESDAY 18

Be careful not to stagnate in your comfort zone

Light is to darkness what love is to fear; in the presence of one the other disappears.

Marianne Williamson

WEDNESDAY 19

As you think, so you act, and react

SEPTEMBER

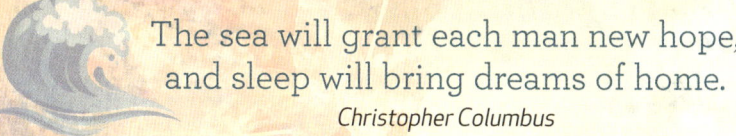

The sea will grant each man new hope,
and sleep will bring dreams of home.
Christopher Columbus

*One ought to look a good deal at oneself
before thinking of condemning others.*
Moliere

THURSDAY 20

Be interested in other people

FRIDAY 21

Volunteer for a local charity

SATURDAY 22

Give to life exactly what you want to get from life

SUNDAY 23

People don't plan to fail, they fail to plan

SEPTEMBER

MONDAY 24

Love is all around

TUESDAY 25

Don't waste new tears on old grief

WEDNESDAY 26

Let go of your fear of criticism

The hallway of every man's life is paced with pictures; pictures gay and pictures gloomy, all useful, for if we be wise, we can learn from them a richer and braver way to live.

Sean O'Casey

> We cling to our point of view as though everything depended on it. Yet our opinions have no permanence; Like autumn and winter, they gradually pass away.
> *Chuang Tzu*

THURSDAY 27

Be willing to fail but committed to succeed

FRIDAY 28

Cross your bridges when you come to them

SATURDAY 29

No person, place or thing has any more power over you than you

SUNDAY 30

Trust yourself to trust others

spriocanna
GOALS

DEIREADH FOMHAIR
OCTOBER

May you be at the gates of heaven an hour before the devil knows you're dead!

Irish proverb

Más maith leat siocháin, cairdeas, agus moladh, éist, feic, agus fan balbh.

If you wish for peace, friendship, and praise, listen, look, and stay silent.

Happiness is neither virtue nor pleasure nor this thing nor that but simply growth. We are happy when we are growing.

WB Yeats

The first to apologise is the bravest,
the first to forgive is the strongest,
and the first to forget is the happiest.

MONDAY **1**

Do as you would be done by

The least movement is of importance to all nature. The entire ocean is affected by a pebble.
Blaise Pascal

TUESDAY **2**

Practice a healthy lifestyle

WEDNESDAY **3**

You become like the people you spend the most time with

THURSDAY **4**

Master your habits or you will be their slave

OCTOBER

> There are two basic motivating forces: fear and love. When we are afraid, we pull back from life. When we are in love, we open to all that life has to offer with passion, excitement, and acceptance.
> *John Lennon*

> *The purpose of all wars is peace.*
> *Saint Augustine*

> We die only once, and for such a long time.
> *Moliere*

FRIDAY 5

Love holds no grievances

SATURDAY 6

Seek first to understand, then to be understood

SUNDAY 7

Celebrate your friendships

Since you are the one who has to live with your choices, be sure they are your own.
Alan Cohen

MONDAY 8

If it's not broken, don't fix it

Sooner or later, everyone sits down to a banquet of consequences.
Robert Louis Stevenson

TUESDAY 9

Take care of your body – it's the only one you have to live in

WEDNESDAY 10

Avoid people who do not encourage you

THURSDAY 11

Only doubtful truths need defence

OCTOBER

What you are in love with, what seizes your imagination, will affect everything. It will decide what will get you out of bed in the mornings, what you will do with your evenings, how you spend your weekends, what you read, who you know, what breaks your heart, and what amazes you with joy and gratitude. Fall in love, stay in love, and it will decide everything.

Pedro Arrupe

FRIDAY 12

Do not dismiss your dreams

SATURDAY 13

Everything you are against weakens you

SUNDAY 14

Negativity keeps you stuck and doesn't change anything

MONDAY **15**

Hope is faith in the future

The ocean stirs the heart, inspires the imagination and brings eternal joy to the soul.
Wyland

TUESDAY **16**

Embrace challenges as access to growth

WEDNESDAY **17**

Discover what excites you and do more of it

THURSDAY **18**

Spend meaningful time with your loved ones (switch off your smartphone!)

FRIDAY **19**

Don't wait, love your life now

OCTOBER

Blessed is he who has learned to admire but not envy, to follow but not imitate, to praise but not flatter, and to lead but not manipulate.
William Arthur Ward

People who think they know everything are a great annoyance to those of us who do.
Isaac Asimov

Letting go is to love yourself enough to look at the past with a different perspective. It is to accept that you can't change the past, but that you can change whether your perspective poisons or nourishes you.
Steve Maraboli

SATURDAY **20**

Things don't matter, people do

SUNDAY **21**

Put pep in your daily step

Life is like a prism. What you see depends on how you turn the glass.
Jonathan Kellerman

The wound is the place where the light enters you.
Rumi

MONDAY 22

Spend money on experiences and collect great memories

TUESDAY 23

Get enough sleep

WEDNESDAY 24

Clear out your fridge

THURSDAY 25

Take a risk that might improve your life

FRIDAY 26

Learn to cook

OCTOBER

Find out what makes you kinder, what opens you up and brings out the most loving, generous, and unafraid version of you – and go after those things as if nothing else matters. Because, actually, nothing else does.

George Saunders

The mind is as big as the universe.
Helen Keller

Inspiration exists, but it has to find us working.
Pablo Picasso

SATURDAY 27

Plan an activity break

SUNDAY 28

Spend time reminiscing with old friends

MONDAY 29
Bank holiday

Stick to the facts – what happened, happened

TUESDAY 30

We complicate life by adding doubt and fear

WEDNESDAY 31

Be proactive

Nothing that is can pause or stay;
The moon will wax, the moon will wane,
The mist and cloud will turn to rain,
The rain to mist and cloud again,
Tomorrow be today.
    Henry Wadsworth Longfellow

All the ills of mankind, all the tragic misfortunes that fill the history books, all the political blunders, all the failures of the great leaders have arisen merely from a lack of skill at dancing.
    Moliere

May you live as long as you want,
And never want as long as you live.
Irish proverb

spriocanna
GOALS
SAMHAIN
NOVEMBER

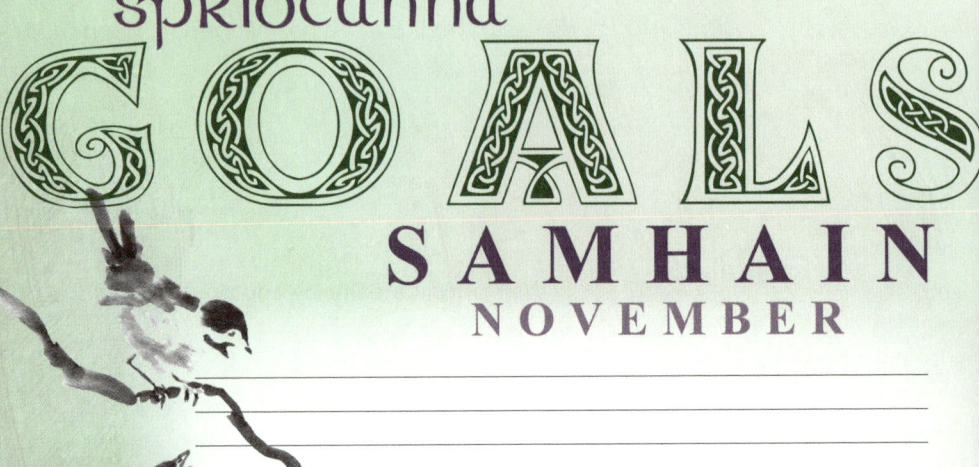

_____
_____
_____
_____
_____
_____
_____
_____
_____

A great source of calamity lies in regret and anticipation; therefore a person is wise who thinks of the present alone, regardless of the past or future.
Oliver Goldsmith

Mol an páiste agus molann tú an mháthair.
Praise the child and you praise the mother.

BE THANKFUL

Courage is like love; it must have hope for nourishment.
Napoleon

Be thankful that you don't already have everything you desire. If you did, what would there be to look forward to?
Be thankful when you don't know something, for it gives you the opportunity to learn.
Be thankful for the difficult times – during those times you grow.
Be thankful for your limitations, because they give you opportunities for improvement.
Be thankful for your mistakes – they will teach you valuable lessons.
Be thankful when you are tired and weary, because it means you worked hard to make a difference.
It is easy to be thankful for the good things. A life of rich fulfilment comes to those who are also thankful for setbacks. Find a way to be thankful for your troubles and they can indeed become your blessings.

THURSDAY 1

It's ok to be happy for no reason

FRIDAY 2

You don't have to believe everything you think, hear, read

NOVEMBER

Success is often the result of taking a misstep in the right direction.
Al Bernstein

SATURDAY **3**

Treat yourself to a 'be nice to me' day

SUNDAY **4**

Relax, you're doing a great job

You want what you don't have and don't want what you already have, and so you suffer. It's perplexing! Why not simply reverse it? Why not want what you have, and not want what you don't have? It's so simple! You can be happy; it's here for the taking.
Nisargadatta Maharaj

We ourselves feel that what we are doing is just a drop in the ocean. But the ocean would be less because of that missing drop.
Mother Teresa

As you start to walk the way, the way appears.
Rumi

You are precisely as big as what you love and precisely as small as what you allow to annoy you.
Robert Anton Wilson

I'm going to make everything around me beautiful – that will be my life.
Elsie de Wolfe

MONDAY 5

Everything is possible in dialogue

TUESDAY 6

Relationships are complicated – ask anyone

WEDNESDAY 7

Your life today is the sum total of all your yesterdays

THURSDAY 8

Be genuinely interested in others

NOVEMBER

> The fact that I can plant a seed and it becomes a flower, share a bit of knowledge and it becomes another's, smile at someone and receive a smile in return, are to me continual spiritual experiences.
> *Leo F Buscaglia*

FRIDAY 9

If you change the way you look at things, the things you look at change

SATURDAY 10

Think kindly of your parents, they are the source of your life

SUNDAY 11

Our beliefs have a lot to answer for – what if they're not true?

Believe. No pessimist ever discovered the secrets of the stars, or sailed to an uncharted island, or opened a new heaven to the human spirit.
Helen Keller

The worst sin toward our fellow creatures is not to hate them, but to be indifferent to them: that's the essence of inhumanity.
  George Bernard Shaw

MONDAY 12

Find the middle way

TUESDAY 13

Think win – win

WEDNESDAY 14

We choose what we listen to

THURSDAY 15

Give thanks for the best thing that happened today

Your only purpose is to be yourself, otherwise you deprive the universe of who you came here to be.
Anita Moorjani

NOVEMBER

I seem to have been only like a boy playing on the seashore, and diverting myself in now and then finding a smoother pebble or a prettier shell than ordinary, whilst the great ocean of truth lay all undiscovered before me.

Isaac Newton

Not everything that is faced can be changed, But nothing can be changed until it is faced.

James A Baldwin

Two roads diverged in a yellow wood,
And sorry I could not travel both

And be one traveler, long I stood
And looked down one as far as I could
To where it bent in the undergrowth;

Then took the other, as just as fair,
And having perhaps the better claim
Because it was grassy and wanted wear...

...Oh, I kept the first for another day!
Yet knowing how way leads on to way
I doubted if I should ever come back.

I shall be telling this with a sigh
Somewhere ages and ages hence:
Two roads diverged in a wood, and I,
I took the one less traveled by,
And that has made all the difference.

Robert Frost

FRIDAY 16

Don't get trapped in negative thinking

**Hold fast to dreams
For if dreams die
Life is a broken-winged bird
That cannot fly.
Hold fast to dreams
For when dreams go
Life is a barren field
Frozen with snow.**
Langston Hughes

One of the greatest gifts you can give to anyone is the gift of your attention.
Jim Rohn

SATURDAY 17

Be your own best friend

SUNDAY 18

In the game of life, be a good sport

NOVEMBER

MONDAY 19

Always keep a sense of humour

TUESDAY 20

Discover your Why and you can figure the How

WEDNESDAY 21

Life is to be enjoyed not endured

Progress is man's ability to complicate simplicity.
Thor Heyerdahl

He is richest who is content with the least, for contentment is the wealth of nature.
Socrates

I can resist everything except temptation.
Oscar Wilde

THURSDAY 22

Be prepared for miracles

FRIDAY 23

Sometimes you just need to let go

SATURDAY 24

Practice to be skilled

SUNDAY 25

Don't wait; the time will never be just right.

You learn more quickly under the guidance of experienced teachers. You waste a lot of time going down blind alleys if you have no one to lead you.
W Somerset Maugham

NOVEMBER

MONDAY 26

Play with the possibilities

TUESDAY 27

Aim for excellence not perfection

WEDNESDAY 28

The greatest wealth is health

THURSDAY 29

Start a fitness routine

FRIDAY 30

It's never wrong to do the right thing

CHRISTMAS SHOPPING LIST

1. Buy a 2019 Get Up and Go Diary for all my friends.

2. Buy a Get Up and Go Travel Journal and plan my next trip.

spriocanna
GOALS

NOLLAIG
DECEMBER

Sláinte chuig na fir agus go maire na mná go deo!

Health to the men and may the women live forever!

_____
_____
_____
_____
_____
_____
_____
_____
_____

May peace and plenty be the first
To lift the latch on your door,
And happiness be guided to your home
By the candle of Christmas.

Irish proverb

The most important things to do in the world
are to get something to eat, something
to drink and somebody to love you.

Brendan Behan

Under the obsessive thoughts and plans, under the emotions, positive and negative, there is an ocean of peace.
Gangaji

SATURDAY 1

Do what nurtures you

There's nothing more beautiful than the way the ocean refuses to stop kissing the shoreline, no matter how many times it's sent away.
Sarah Kay

Stop thinking of the extremes, good and bad, right and wrong. Rather look at yourself in the moment. Observe intelligently, without any comments, without any reactions. Do not be for or against anything. Stay centered.
Robert Adams

SUNDAY 2

Be your own super hero

DECEMBER

Instead of seeing imperfections, choose to see the light that exists in everyone. Too often we focus on what we see physically with our eyesight and don't use our insight to see something more significant in the soul of another.

While it is well enough to leave footprints on the sands of time, it is even more important to make sure they point in a commendable direction.
— James Branch Cabell

MONDAY 3

Get enough sleep

TUESDAY 4

Spend time having fun with friends

WEDNESDAY 5

Begin with the end in mind

> *You have been criticising yourself for years and it hasn't worked. Try approving of yourself and see what happens.*
> Louise L Hay

THURSDAY 6

Participate in a fun activity – just for fun

FRIDAY 7

Go the extra mile

SATURDAY 8

We find what we look for

SUNDAY 9

Don't give up

Next time you are struggling with something, try treating yourself like a good friend and see what happens.

DECEMBER

The only way that we can live is if we grow
The only way that we can grow is if we change
The only way we can change is if we learn
The only way we can learn is if we are exposed
The only way we can become exposed is if we throw ourselves out into the open.
Do it. Throw yourself.

To be beautiful means to be yourself. You don't need to be accepted by others. You need to accept yourself. When you are born a lotus flower, be a beautiful lotus flower, don't try to be a magnolia flower. If you crave acceptance and recognition and try to change yourself to fit what other people want you to be, you will suffer all your life. True happiness and true power lie in understanding yourself, accepting yourself, having confidence in yourself.

Thích Nhat Hanh

MONDAY **10**

Visualise your success

> It is not what they profess but what they practice that makes them good.
> *Greek Proverb*

TUESDAY 11

Everyone makes mistakes

> If everyone were clothed with integrity, if every heart were just, frank, kindly, the other virtues would be well-nigh useless.
> *Moliere*

> *Your resistance to change is your fear of the death of who you think you are. Actually, change destroys who you are not, so who you are can emerge.*
> *P Rengel*

WEDNESDAY 12

Be open to contribution from others

THURSDAY 13

Acknowledge your personal best

DECEMBER

> If you have only one smile in you, give it to the people you love. Don't be surly at home, then go out in the street and start grinning "Good morning" at total strangers.
> *Maya Angelou*

> *Art is the lie that enables us to realise the truth.*
> *Pablo Picasso*

FRIDAY 14

You can fool your mind but not your body

SATURDAY 15

Put first things first

SUNDAY 16

Don't stand in your own way

Human beings are works in progress that mistakenly think they're finished.

MONDAY **17**

Become a positive role model for others

Lives of great men all remind us, we can make our lives sublime, and, departing, leave behind us, footprints on the sands of time.
Henry Wadsworth Longfellow

TUESDAY **18**

Develop healthy daily routines

WEDNESDAY **19**

Make the first move

THURSDAY **20**

All you give is given to yourself

DECEMBER

Do not worry about tomorrow. for tomorrow will worry about itself. Today has enough troubles of its own.

FRIDAY 21

Love your enemies; you learn from them

Success is not the key to happiness. Happiness is the key to success. If you love what your are doing, you are already successful.

SATURDAY 22

Your best is always good enough

SUNDAY 23

Believe in yourself

There is joy in self-forgetfulness. So I try to make the light in others' eyes my sun, the music in others' ears my symphony, the smile on others' lips my happiness.
Helen Keller

MONDAY 24

If it feels good, do it!

Honesty has a beautiful and refreshing simplicity about it. No ulterior motives. No hidden meanings. An absence of hypocrisy, duplicity, political games and verbal superiority. As honesty and real integrity characterise our lives, there will be no need to manipulate others.
Charles Swindoll

When anxious, uneasy and bad thoughts come, I go to the sea, and the sea drowns them out with its great wide sounds, cleanses me with its noise, and imposes a rhythm upon everything in me that is bewildered and confused.
Rainer Maria Rilke

DECEMBER

A CHRISTMAS BLESSING

During this Christmas season,
may you be blessed
with the spirit of the season
which is peace;
the gladness of the season
which is hope;
and the heart of the season
which is love.

It's not what's under the tree that matters; it's who is gathered around it.

Merry Christmas
Happy New Year

TUESDAY 25
Christmas Day

Merry Christmas!

WEDNESDAY 26

Be kind to everyone you meet

THURSDAY 27

Make the most of what you have

Take the time to feed a goldfish, walk a dog, stroke a cat, groom a horse, listen to a bird.

FRIDAY 28

Be willing to forgive

SATURDAY 29

Don't lose sight of your dreams

SUNDAY 30

Keep a journal

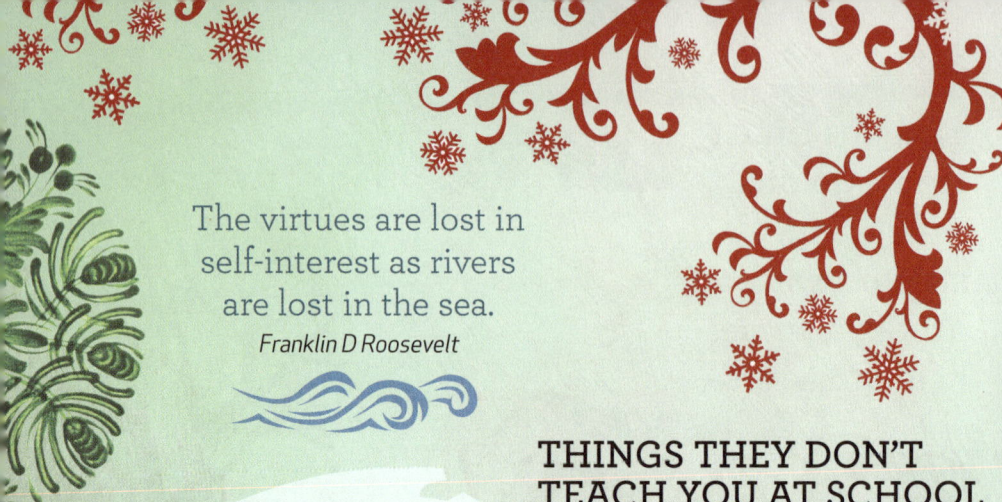

The virtues are lost in self-interest as rivers are lost in the sea.
Franklin D Roosevelt

Program your mind for success and achievement by visualising what you want. Being a winner is an attitude, a self-concept, a way of life.

THINGS THEY DON'T TEACH YOU AT SCHOOL
How to love somebody.
How to be famous.
How to be rich or how to be poor.
How to walk away from someone you don't love any longer.
How to know what's going on in someone else's mind.
What to say to someone who's dying.
They don't teach you anything worth knowing.

MONDAY 31

Relax; everything will work out for the best

The most beautiful world is always entered through imagination.
Helen Keller

DESIDERATA

Go placidly amid the noise and haste, and remember what peace there may be in silence. As far as possible without surrender be on good terms with all persons. Speak your truth quietly and clearly, and listen to others, even the dull and ignorant; they too have their story.

Avoid loud and aggressive persons, they are vexations to the spirit. If you compare yourself with others, you may become vain and bitter; for always there will be greater and lesser persons than yourself. Enjoy your achievements as well as your plans. Keep interested in your own career, however humble; it is a real possession in the changing fortunes of time. Exercise caution in your business affairs; for the world is full of trickery. But let this not blind you to what virtue there is; many persons strive for high ideals; and everywhere life is full of heroism.

Be yourself. Especially, do not feign affection. Neither be cynical about love; for in the face of all aridity and disenchantment it is perennial as the grass. Take kindly the counsel of the years, gracefully surrendering the things of youth. Nurture strength of spirit to shield you in sudden misfortune. But do not distress yourself with imaginings. Many fears are born of fatigue and loneliness. Beyond a wholesome discipline, be gentle with yourself.

You are a child of the universe, no less than the trees and the stars; you have a right to be here. And whether or not it is clear to you, no doubt the universe is unfolding as it should. Therefore be at peace with God, whatever you conceive Him to be; and whatever your labours and aspirations, in the noisy confusion of life keep peace with your soul. With all its sham, drudgery and broken dreams, it is still a beautiful world. Be cheerful. Strive to be happy.

Max Ehrmann

2019 CALENDAR

JANAURY

Mo	Tu	We	Th	Fr	Sa	Su
	1	2	3	4	5	6
7	8	9	10	11	12	13
14	15	16	17	18	19	20
21	22	23	24	25	26	27
28	29	30	31			

FEBRUARY

Mo	Tu	We	Th	Fr	Sa	Su
				1	2	3
4	5	6	7	8	9	10
11	12	13	14	15	16	17
18	19	20	21	22	23	24
25	26	27	28			

MARCH

Mo	Tu	We	Th	Fr	Sa	Su
				1	2	3
4	5	6	7	8	9	10
11	12	13	14	15	16	17
18	19	20	21	22	23	24
25	26	27	28	29	30	31

APRIL

Mo	Tu	We	Th	Fr	Sa	Su
1	2	3	4	5	6	7
8	9	10	11	12	13	14
15	16	17	18	19	20	21
22	23	24	25	26	27	28
29	30					

MAY

Mo	Tu	We	Th	Fr	Sa	Su
		1	2	3	4	5
6	7	8	9	10	11	12
13	14	15	16	17	18	19
20	21	22	23	24	25	26
27	28	29	30	31		

JUNE

Mo	Tu	We	Th	Fr	Sa	Su
					1	2
3	4	5	6	7	8	9
10	11	12	13	14	15	16
17	18	19	20	21	22	23
24	25	26	27	28	29	30

JULY

Mo	Tu	We	Th	Fr	Sa	Su
1	2	3	4	5	6	7
8	9	10	11	12	13	14
15	16	17	18	19	20	21
22	23	24	25	26	27	28
29	30	31				

AUGUST

Mo	Tu	We	Th	Fr	Sa	Su
			1	2	3	4
5	6	7	8	9	10	11
12	13	14	15	16	17	18
19	20	21	22	23	24	25
26	27	28	29	30	31	

SEPTEMBER

Mo	Tu	We	Th	Fr	Sa	Su
						1
2	3	4	5	6	7	8
9	10	11	12	13	14	15
16	17	18	19	20	21	22
23	24	25	26	27	28	29
30						

OCTOBER

Mo	Tu	We	Th	Fr	Sa	Su
	1	2	3	4	5	6
7	8	9	10	11	12	13
14	15	16	17	18	19	20
21	22	23	24	25	26	27
28	29	30	31			

NOVEMBER

Mo	Tu	We	Th	Fr	Sa	Su
				1	2	3
4	5	6	7	8	9	10
11	12	13	14	15	16	17
18	19	20	21	22	23	24
25	26	27	28	29	30	

DECEMBER

Mo	Tu	We	Th	Fr	Sa	Su
						1
2	3	4	5	6	7	8
9	10	11	12	13	14	15
16	17	18	19	20	21	22
23	24	25	26	27	28	29
30	31					

INTRODUCING OUR LATEST PUBLICATION

Get Up and Go Heroes

These 24 real-life stories from Get Up and Go Publications Ltd shed a revealing light on how people overcome extraordinary challenges and keep going even when nothing seems to be working.

From extraordinary and moving situations, to moments and decisions that change the trajectory of a life, the pieces in this book give revealing insights into how to overcame difficulty. Some experiences are a gift and others a lesson. At times the lesson simply is that apparent failure is the universe's way of nudging you to make changes.

Many of us believe that we need to be extraordinary to achieve great things, but, as this book shows, heroes are ordinary people 'given being and action by something bigger than themselves'.

The book was launched at the 2017 Get Up and Go event in Sligo, Ireland – Get Up and Go with Passion and Purpose.

The contributors have either been speakers at previous Get Up and Go Events, or potential speakers at future events, as they each have an inspirational message to share, with an intention to empower, motivate and encourage you, the reader, to 'get up and go' forward in your own life.

The annual Get Up and Go event is not for profit and all proceeds from Get Up and Go Heroes will be donated to Cystic Fibrosis Ireland, Pieta House, Northwest Simon and CHAB School Cambodia.

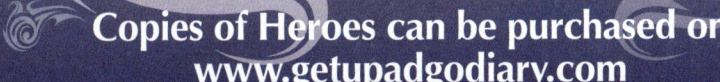

Copies of Heroes can be purchased on
www.getupadgodiary.com

Follow us on our Facebook page Get Up and Go Events
for details of future events.

FOR MORE COPIES VISIT OUR WEBSITE
www.getupandgodiary.com

OR CONTACT US ON
info@getupandgodiary.com

Postal address: **Get Up and Go Publications Ltd, Camboline, Hazelwood, Sligo, Ireland F91 NP04.**

DIRECT ORDER FORM (please complete by ticking boxes)
PLEASE SEND ME:

- The Irish Get Up and Go Diary **2018** ☐ **2019** ☐ €10/£9   Quantity ____
- The Irish Get Up and Go Diary (case bound) **2018** ☐ **2019** ☐ €15/£13   Quantity ____
- Get Up and Go Diary for Busy Women **2018** ☐ **2019** ☐ €10/£9   Quantity ____
- Get Up and Go Diary for Busy Women (case bound) **2018** ☐ **2019** ☐ €15/£13   Quantity ____
- Get Up and Go Diary **2018** ☐ **2019** ☐ €10/£9   Quantity ____
- Get Up and Go Diary for Girls **2018** ☐ **2019** ☐ €10/£9   Quantity ____
- Get Up and Go Diary for Boys **2018** ☐ **2019** ☐ €10/£9   Quantity ____
- Get Up and Go Travel Journal ☐ €12/£10.50   Quantity ____
- Get Up and Go Genius Journal ☐ €15/£13   Quantity ____
- Get Up and Go Student Journal (homework journal) ☐ €14/£12   Quantity ____
- Get Up and Go Heroes (all proceeds to charity) ☐ €10/£9   Quantity ____
- The Confidence to Succeed (by Donna Kennedy) ☐ €12.50/£10   Quantity ____

Total number of copies ____

P+P WITHIN IRELAND €2.50 PER COPY.
P+P INTERNATIONAL/OVERSEAS €3.50 PER COPY.

I enclose cheque/postal order for (total amount including P+P): _____

Name: _____

Address: _____

_____

Contact phone number: _____   Email: _____

For orders over eight items, please contact us on 086 1788631 / 071 9146717